MAKE it WORK!

DINOSAURS

Andrew Haslam

written by
Dr. Mike Benton

Consultant: Dr. Arthur Cruickshank
Honorary Research Assistant at Leicestershire Museum

WORLD BOOK / TWO-CAN

MAKE it WORK!
Other titles

First published in the United States in 1996 by
World Book Inc.
525 W. Monroe
20th Floor
Chicago IL USA 60661
in association with Two-Can Publishing Ltd.

Copyright © Two-Can Publishing Ltd, 1996
Series concept and original design © Andrew Haslam and Wendy Baker

**For information on other World Book products,
call 1-800-255-1750, x 2238.**

ISBN: 0-7166-1756-0 (pbk.)
ISBN: 0-7166-1755-2 (hbk.)
LC: 96-60455

Printed in Hong Kong

1 2 3 4 5 6 7 8 9 10 99 98 97 96

Text: Dr. Michael Benton
Editor: Jennet Stott
Senior Designer: Lisa Nutt
Managing Designer: Helen McDonagh
Project Editor: Kate Graham
Managing Editor: Christine Morley
Managing Art Director: Carole Orbell
Photography: John Englefield
Production: Joya Bart-Plange

Contents

Words marked in **bold** in the text are explained in the glossary.

A person who studies **dinosaurs** is called a **paleontologist**. Paleontologists work like detectives, uncovering clues to the past by digging for **skeletons** and **fossils**. By studying dinosaurs, we can begin to understand what the world was like millions of years ago.

MAKE it WORK!

In this book we show you how to make lots of dinosaur models. These help you to understand how their bodies worked, how strong their bones were, and how fast they moved. The models are painted in various colors. Although no one knows what colors dinosaurs really were, we have used camouflage shades, such as green and yellow, for the plant-eaters, and bright shades for the meat-eaters.

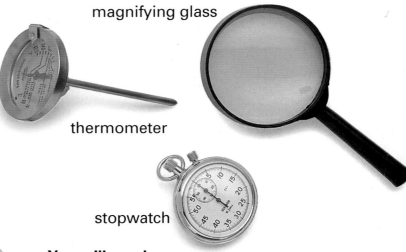

magnifying glass

thermometer

stopwatch

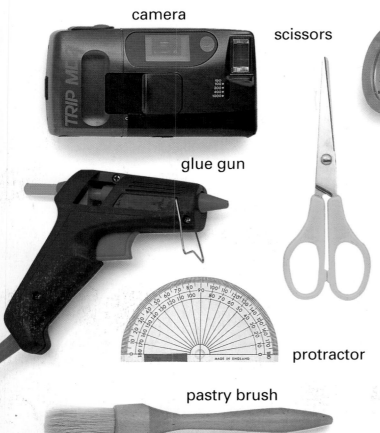

camera

scissors

glue gun

protractor

pastry brush

paintbrush

You will need

You can make most of the models out of simple materials, such as cardboard, wood, plastic bottles, and wire. You will also need a craft knife and scissors to cut some of the materials. Throughout the book, we mention enlarging shapes on a photocopier. You may have to ask an adult to help you with this.

pencil sharpener

ruler

notepad and pencil

Paleontologists use many different scientific techniques in their work. When they find a dinosaur skeleton, they remove the rock that surrounds it. To do this, they use special tools to pick away at the rock, or chemicals, such as acid, to dissolve it.

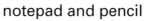

Safety!
If you are using sharp tools, remember that they can be very dangerous! Be careful when you use them and ask an adult to help you. Make sure that anything you are cutting or drilling is held firmly, so that it cannot slip.

hacksaw

Making dinosaurs to scale
The models in this book are made to a scale of about 1:30. This means that the dinosaurs would be 30 times longer and taller in real life.

hand drill

belt punch

clamp

pliers

screwdriver

bradawl

tenon saw

hammer

Keeping records
Paleontologists work very slowly and carefully. They keep detailed records of every stage of their work with photographs, drawings and notes. It doesn't matter if you don't have a camera. Using a notebook to draw and write about your finds is an excellent way of keeping a record.

Naming dinosaurs
When paleontologists discover a new dinosaur, they give it a name. This name is often made up of Latin and Greek words that describe the dinosaur. So, *Tyrannosaurus rex* means "tyrant reptile king." The first name—*Tyrannosaurus*—is the name of the **genus** (group with the same characteristics). The second name—*rex*—is the name of the **species**.

The Earth is about 4,600 million years old. Life appeared about 3,500 million years ago in the form of tiny single **cells**, something like viruses. Fossils of these cells can be seen only under a micro-scope. Dinosaurs first roamed the Earth 225 million years ago and humans emerged less than 5 million years ago!

To make a clock

1 Using a compass, draw a circle 8 in. in diameter on green cardboard, then cut it out. Now make a hole in the middle of the circle.

2 Use a protractor to divide the circle into 12 equal divisions. Mark each one with a short line in white pencil. Stencil on the numbers 1 to 12 for the hours with yellow paint. At each hour, stencil the number of years in white paint using the clock below as a guide. Each hour represents one-twelfth of 4,600 million years.

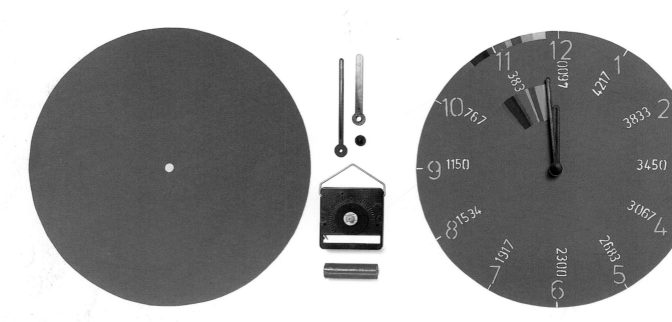

MAKE it WORK!

Make yourself a **geological** time scale. You can make a clock or a time chart. The 12 hours of the clock face represent the age of the Earth from 4,600 million years ago to the present. It shows that dinosaurs appeared in the last hour and humans in the last few seconds.

You will need

glue	a compass
scissors	a protractor
stencils	colored pencils
a paper fastener	colored cardboard
paints and paintbrushes	
a clock motor with battery, hands, nut and plastic cap	

3 Draw a line to mark the beginning of the past 570 million years. From this line up to the number 12 (present day), you will need to paint colored strips representing the different geological periods shown opposite. Each color represents a different period. The colors should follow the order shown in the time chart opposite.

4 Remove the nut and the hands from the central spindle of the clock motor. Put the spindle through the hole in the clock face from the back of the cardboard. Replace the nut on the spindle, then put the hands on. Fit the plastic cap over the hands. If you don't have a clock motor, use a paper fastener to attach the hands.

To make a time strip

1 Take a 6 1/2 ft. length of green cardboard. Starting with 0 at the top, divide it into periods of 100 million years using thin strips of red tape, as shown right. Each 100-million-year period should be 2 in. deep.

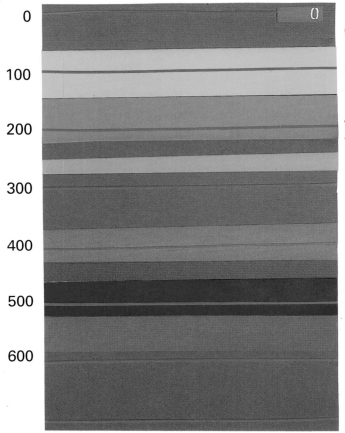

Millions of years   Geological periods

Millions of years	Geological periods
0	Cenozoic
100	**Cretaceous**
200	**Jurassic**
	Triassic
	Permian
300	Carboniferous
400	Devonian
	Silurian
500	Ordovician
	Cambrian
600	

2 Using the colors in the picture above as your guide, cut out thin strips of cardboard of varying widths—these mark the geological periods of the past 570 million years. Glue the strips of cardboard to the top end of the green strip, following the order of colors above. Now label each 1,000-million-year period with red cardboard.

Dinosaurs lived during the Triassic, Jurassic and Cretaceous periods. Triassic dinosaurs included Coelophysis *and* Plateosaurus. *Stegosaurus and* Brachiosaurus *lived during the Jurassic period.* Triceratops *and* Deinonychus *lived during the Cretaceous period.*

We know that dinosaurs existed because their fossil bones and footprints have been found. Fossils, the preserved remains of ancient plants and animals, are often found in rock. When a dinosaur died, the soft parts of its body rotted away, leaving only the bones and teeth. Some skeletons were preserved in layers of sand and mud. **Minerals** carried in water soaked into the bones and, over millions of years, turned them to stone.

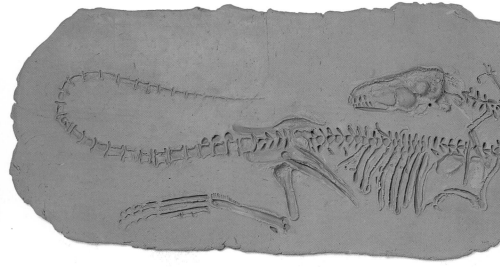

MAKE it WORK!

Make your own model of a fossil dinosaur skeleton, and then make a cast—a shape created by pressing material into a mold. This is the fossil of a theropod, a two-legged meat-eater from the Late Triassic.

You will need

a pushpin
a pencil
plasticine
tracing paper
a modeling knife   a rolling pin
a cardboard box   plaster of Paris

1 Roll out a large piece of plasticine until it makes an even slab about $1/3$ in. thick. Make sure the surface of the plasticine is smooth and even, as any cracks or marks may spoil the look of your finished cast.

2 Trace the skeleton of the dinosaur shown opposite, then enlarge it on a photocopier. Lay the enlarged photocopy on top of the plasticine sheet and prick through the paper with a pushpin to mark the outline of the dinosaur on the plasticine. Lift the photocopy off and use the modeling knife to join the dots and shape the outline of the dinosaur. Then carve the bones neatly out of the plasticine.

3 Make a frame for the mold by cutting off the base of a cardboard box. The rectangular frame should be at least 2 in. deep.

4 Press the frame into the mold. Make sure no gaps are left between the plasticine and the sides of the frame.

5 Mix up some plaster of Paris (it should be pourable, but not watery). Pour it into the frame, so that it completely covers the plasticine and forms a layer $1/3$-$2/3$ in. deep. Let the plaster harden.

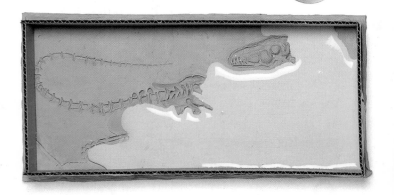

6 Carefully peel off the plasticine to reveal the cast (you can use the mold again to make another cast). Flip the plaster over and you should have a perfect dinosaur cast.

Dinosaur fossils look very different from the flesh and blood creatures that walked the Earth millions of years ago. In the fossil model above, for example, the neck is bent back because all the **ligaments** have dried up.

When an animal dies, its body usually breaks down quickly. In the first four weeks, fluids, such as blood, disappear. Within a year, all soft tissues, such as flesh, will have decomposed. In one to two years, the collagen, or bone protein, is lost. Only if the body is quickly covered in sediment, such as sand or mud, does it stand a chance of being preserved.

ammonite
fossil

leaf fossil

Ammonites were a type of shellfish. Their fossils are found in rocks formed millions of years ago during Jurassic and Cretaceous times. Their coiled shells are among the fossils most often found.

Fossilized plants, such as the leaf above, are usually found in limestone and sandstone rocks, or in coal deposits. Coal deposits are the remains of forests that rotted down millions of years ago, and were covered by many layers of sand or mud.

10 The Dinosaur World

When dinosaurs were alive, the world was much warmer than it is today. There were three main ages of dinosaurs—the Triassic, Jurassic and Cretaceous. Different dinosaurs lived during each of these times, and a variety of plants and other animals existed alongside them.

▲ Triassic—hot, dry, vast deserts

MAKE it WORK!

Make your own dinosaur landscapes and put plastic dinosaur models in them. Find out which dinosaurs lived when (the chart on pages 6 and 7 will help you) and put them in the landscape for that period. Add plastic palm trees to the landscapes, or make your own trees.

You will need

paints	tape
scissors	glue
thin green cardboard	dried moss
plaster of Paris	newspapers
wooden skewers	strips of cloth
plastic dinosaur models	
three wooden boards 12 x 18 in.	

1 Build a landscape on each board by crumpling newspaper into different shapes as shown below. Give the Triassic landscape large mountains and add a volcano to the Cretaceous landscape. Tape to hold the newspaper firmly in place.

2 Mix some plaster of Paris in a bowl to make a very wet paste. Soak strips of cloth in this paste.

3 Spread the cloth strips over each landscape frame you have made. Smooth the surface carefully with your hands and let dry.

▲ Jurassic—warm, with lush vegetation

4 Make the Triassic landscape look like a desert by using orange, red and yellow paint. Paint the Jurassic landscape with green, brown and yellow paint to look like plants and soil. Add rivers and lakes with blue paint to both. Paint the bare, volcanic landscape of the Cretaceous with shades of brown, yellow and purple paint.

▼ Triassic
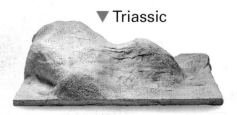

▼ Jurassic
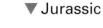

▼ Cretaceous

5 To make your own trees, cut out a rectangle of lightweight green cardboard $2^{1}/_{4}$ x $1^{1}/_{8}$ in. Make 20 equally-spaced cuts along one long side of the cardboard. Glue the uncut edge around the top of a skewer and spread the leaves.

6 Make 20 palm trees and push them into the landscapes. If you are using model palm trees, glue these to the landscapes at this point.

7 Make some bushes with the dried moss and glue them to each of the landscapes, especially along the river banks. The Triassic deserts should be scattered with thin bushes, while the Jurassic landscape should have plenty of large bushes. The landscapes are now ready for your dinosaurs.

8 Arrange the dinosaur models so that the plant-eaters are feeding from the tops of the palm trees or from the low bushes. Some of the meat-eaters could be lurking behind the trees, ready to pounce on their prey.

The dinosaur world was very different from our own. When dinosaurs first appeared, the great land masses were all joined together. They later drifted apart to their present positions. Climates were hotter since there were no polar ice caps. Triassic dinosaurs lived in hot, dry conditions, but the climate became wetter in the Jurassic and Cretaceous.

▶ Cretaceous—warm, with volcanoes in some areas

12 What is a Dinosaur?

Dinosaurs were **reptiles** that lived only on land. They could not fly, nor could they live in water. They belonged to the **Archosauria**, or "ruling reptiles" group. This group includes ancient flying reptiles, or **pterosaurs**, as well as present-day crocodiles and birds. All dinosaurs lived during the **Mesozoic** era, 250 million to 65 million years ago.

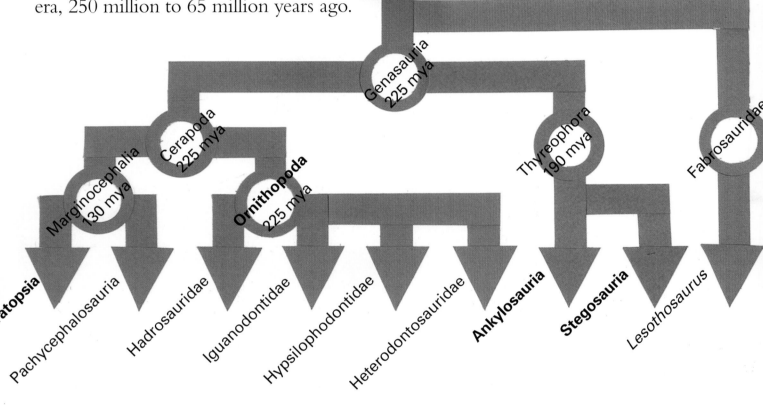

mya = million years ago

Dinosauria 235 mya

Ornithischia 230 mya

Genasauria 225 mya

Cerapoda 225 mya

Marginocephalia 130 mya

Ornithopoda 225 mya

Thyreophora 190 mya

Fabrosauridae

Ceratopsia

Pachycephalosauria

Hadrosauridae

Iguanodontidae

Hypsilophodontidae

Heterodontosauridae

Ankylosauria

Stegosauria

Lesothosaurus

MAKE it WORK!
This model of the dinosaur evolutionary tree shows how dinosaurs evolved over 160 million years on Earth and which types are most closely related. After making your tree, add plastic dinosaurs in their correct positions.

You will need
a pencil
a compass
colored cardboard
scissors and glue
wooden baseboard 12 x 12 in.

1 Make the tree as shown above, using colored cardboard. Put it together on the baseboard and glue in place. Add the names of the dinosaur groups on cards and arrange your plastic models on the correct "branch" of the tree.

The branches of the evolutionary tree
At the top of the tree is Dinosauria—the whole class of dinosaurs. Below it are the two main groups of dinosaurs—the Ornithischia and the Saurischia. **Ornithischian** dinosaurs have birdlike hips. **Saurischian** dinosaurs have lizardlike hips.

Putting dinosaurs into groups

Ornithischian dinosaurs are all plant-eaters and some of them, such as *Triceratops*, have horns, spines and other kinds of armor. Saurischians include the meat-eating **theropods** and the long-necked, plant-eating **sauropods**.

Once you know whether a dinosaur is a Saurischian or Ornithischian, you need to find out what kind of skeleton it has to move further down the tree. For example, dinosaurs are placed in different groups according to the shape and structure of their skulls or backbones. Some of this information can be very difficult to find, especially without a complete skeleton to study.

look up bold names in the glossary on pages 46 to 47

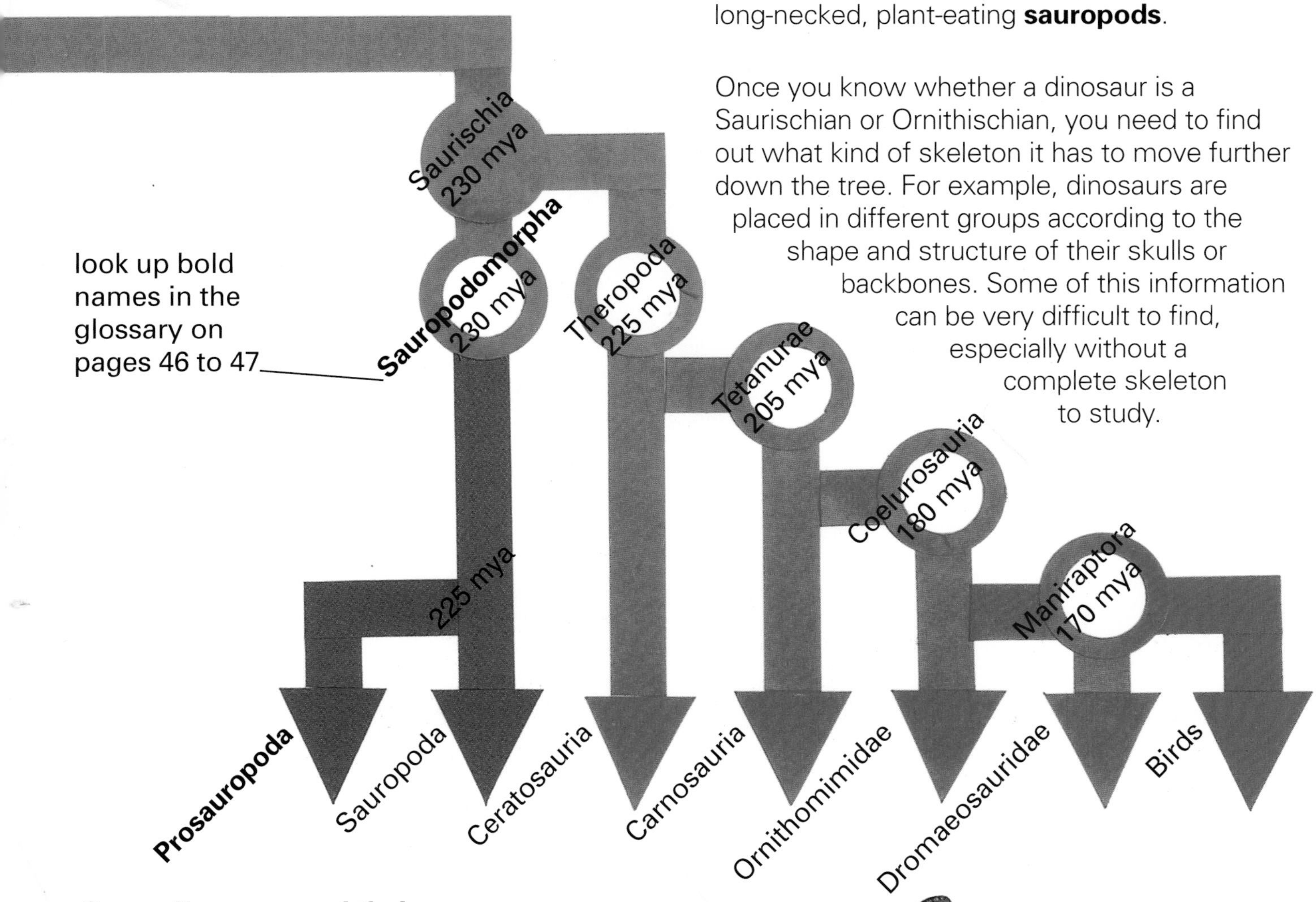

Saurischia 230 mya

Sauropodomorpha 230 mya

Theropoda 225 mya

Tetanurae 205 mya

Coelurosauria 180 mya

Maniraptora 170 mya

225 mya

Prosauropoda

Sauropoda

Ceratosauria

Carnosauria

Ornithomimidae

Dromaeosauridae

Birds

Some dinosaurs and their groups

Triceratops
● Ceratopsia

Iguanodon
● Iguanodontidae

Scelidosaurus
● Thyreophora

Stegosaurus
● Stegosauria

Apatosaurus
● Sauropoda

Brachiosaurus
● Sauropoda

Diplodocus
● Sauropoda

Tyrannosaurus
● Carnosauria

14 Digging up Dinosaurs

Dozens of dinosaur skeletons are dug up every year. Paleontologists search for them along ancient rivers, lakes and desert dunes. An **excavation** may be sparked off by the discovery of a few small bone pieces that have been washed out of the ground by rain or floods. Months of digging may follow to find out if there is a whole skeleton buried, or just a few fragments.

To make the drawing

1 Carefully place the cast you have already made on a photocopier and make a copy of it. Using thin tape, make a grid of 1/2 in. squares over the photocopy as shown in the picture below (paleontologists use grids to make their drawings more accurate).

2 Trace the dinosaur from the photocopy using the grid squares as a guide. Once you have completed the tracing, add a white and red line to show the scale—each block represents about 3 ft. Glue the drawing onto a piece of white cardboard as shown.

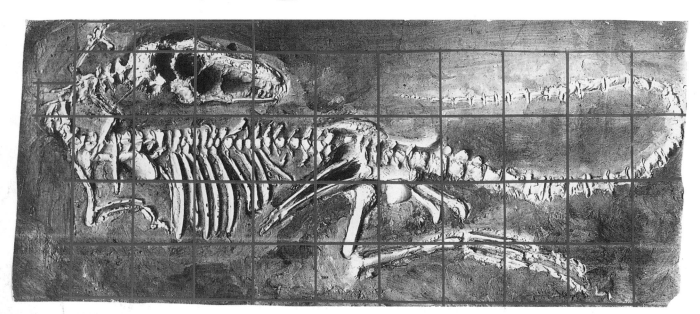

MAKE it WORK!

When a skeleton is discovered, paleontologists work on site, first photographing the skeleton and then drawing it. Here we show you how to draw a grid of a meat-eating dinosaur cast and make a model excavation site. First you will need to make the fossil cast on pages 8 and 9.

You will need

fine sand	a dowel rod
red thread	scissors
a craft knife	tracing paper
modeling clay	pushpins and tape
a drinking straw	a small hammer
green and white cardboard	a modeling knife
paints and paintbrushes	a ruler and a pencil

To make the excavation site

1 Use modeling clay to build soil and rocks around the dinosaur cast to make it look like an excavation site. Sprinkle fine sand all over the surface, except on the skeleton, and press it into the clay.

2 To make the grid, lay a ruler across the area immediately surrounding, and over, the skeleton. Using a small hammer, gently knock pushpins in at regular intervals. Take care not to crack the surrounding plaster. Tie lengths of red thread between the pushpins to make a model grid, just like a paleontologist's grid. Place a drinking straw at the back of the grid to act as a surveyor's pole.

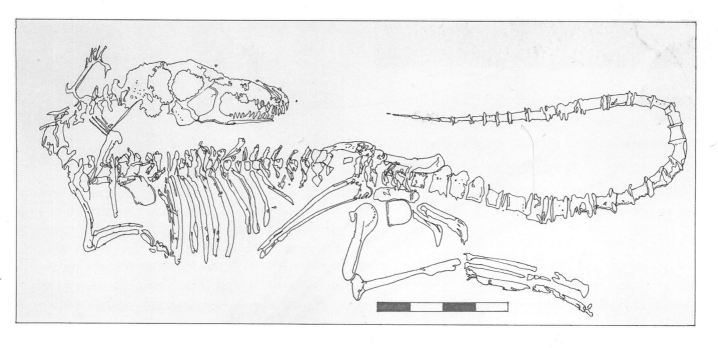

3 Add model trees to the site, or make them using various lengths of dowel rod for trunks. Use green cardboard for the leaves (see page 11 for instructions on how to make them). Push the trees into the clay on the board and build up clay around the base to fix them in place.

4 Paint the edges of the plaster base to look like sand and soil. Place model people at the site—these are the paleontologists.

Digging up a dinosaur skeleton is a huge task. It might take a team of five to 10 paleontologists several weeks to carefully dig up all the pieces. A complete skeleton can weigh 22 short tons or more.

Dinosaur skeletons contain hundreds of bones, just as ours do. In fact, you can match the shape and position of most dinosaur bones with bones in human skeletons. Like us, dinosaurs had skulls, backbones, and arm and leg bones.

MAKE it WORK!

Make a large, simple skeleton of a four-legged dinosaur. This is a model of *Apatosaurus*, one of the biggest dinosaurs. It was a plant-eater that may have weighed as much as 33 short tons.

You will need

a craft knife
tracing paper
masking tape
corrugated cardboard
colored gummed labels

1 Trace the outlines of all the bones shown at right. Enlarge the backbone until it is 3 1/2 ft. long. Then enlarge the other pieces by the same percentage.

2 Lay the tracings over the cardboard. To prevent the tracings from sliding as you cut, tape them to the cardboard with masking tape. Ask an adult to help you cut out the shapes with a craft knife, then remove the paper tracings. Cut slits 1 1/3 in. long in the shapes, as shown at right.

3 Number the colored gummed labels and stick them to the bone shapes in the positions shown.

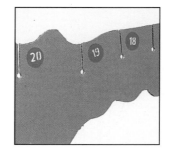 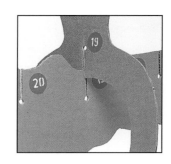

4 The neck and backbone are made out of one piece of cardboard. Push the rib sections with red labels numbered 12 to 20 into the matching red slots along the backbone, as shown above. Make sure the rib sections are in the right order: the ribs should be longest in the middle of the backbone, and become shorter as they reach the front of the neck.

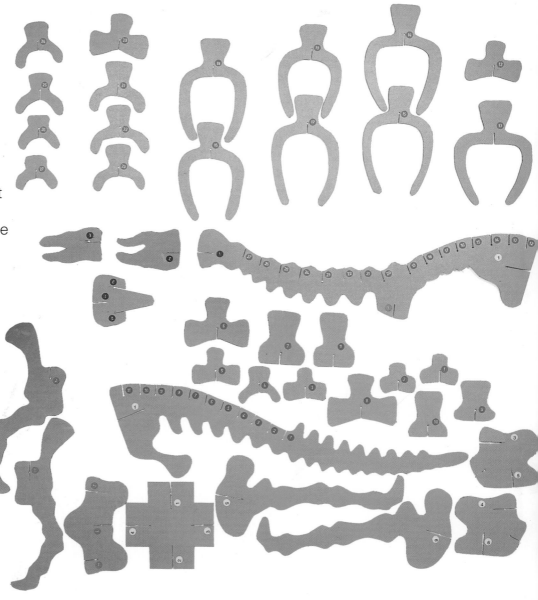

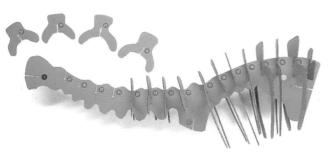

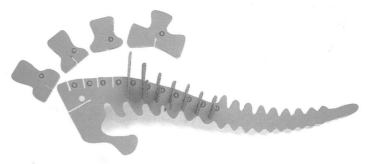

5 Slot the remaining rib sections with red labels numbered 21 to 27 into the front of the neck and backbone, as shown above.

8 Fit the rib sections with red labels numbered 1 to 11 onto the tail region as shown above. Now put all the pieces together as shown below and slot the two halves of the skeleton together.

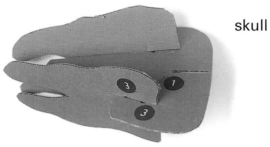

skull

6 Make the skull by slotting together the three skull pieces with blue labels numbered 1 to 3. Make sure the pieces are pushed into the slots with the matching numbers.

7 Now make up the front legs with green-labeled pieces numbered 1 to 3 and back legs with yellow-labeled pieces numbered 1 to 6. Make sure the legs face in the right direction. Adjust the final fitting of the legs when the model is complete to make it stand steady.

Dinosaurs like Apatosaurus *had up to 450 bones. There were dozens of bones in the backbone and just as many in the tail. Two ribs were attached to each bone in the backbone, and there were up to 50 or 60 bones in the skull.*

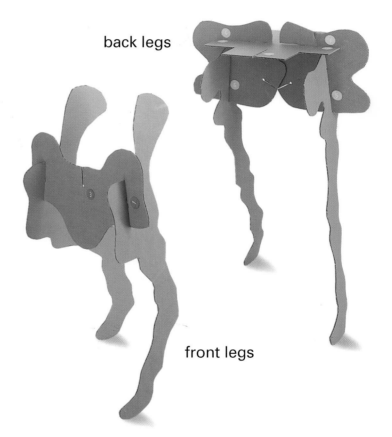

back legs

front legs

How the skeleton works

Dinosaur skeletons had to support a lot of weight, so they had to be very strong. The leg bones of a large dinosaur, for example, had to be thick enough to bear the dinosaur's enormous weight without breaking. Although the bones were thick, the skeleton was designed so that the animal could move freely.

You have made a model of the skeleton of the *Apatosaurus*, one of the largest dinosaurs that ever lived. It weighed 10 times as much as an elephant! Now you can look at each part of the *Apatosaurus* skeleton to see how such an enormous animal worked.

The backbone and legs

The backbone and the legs are the engineering marvels of the giant sauropods. In *Apatosaurus,* the distance between the shoulder and the hips is quite short. Notice how the backbone arches up to give it the strength to hold the weight of all the internal organs inside the ribcage. The backbone is particularly strong in the hip region.

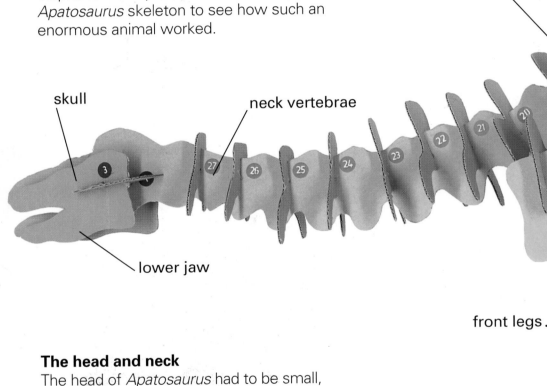

shoulder blade

skull

neck vertebrae

lower jaw

front legs

The head and neck

The head of *Apatosaurus* had to be small, otherwise the long neck would never have been able to support it (animals with large heads have short necks). Still, with such a small mouth, it is difficult to see how *Apatosaurus* could eat enough to feed its huge body.

Paleontologists believe that *Apatosaurus* moved its neck slowly from side to side in search of food. It could probably raise its neck a little to grab leaves from the trees. The long neck worked like a crane. It was probably moved by powerful muscles and ligaments along the top of the neck, rather like the steel cables that move the arm of a crane.

The spines on the backbone are very high around the hips—sometimes as much as $1\frac{1}{2}$ ft. in height. This would have provided support for the strong muscles and ligaments that helped the backbone carry the weight of the stomach and other internal organs.

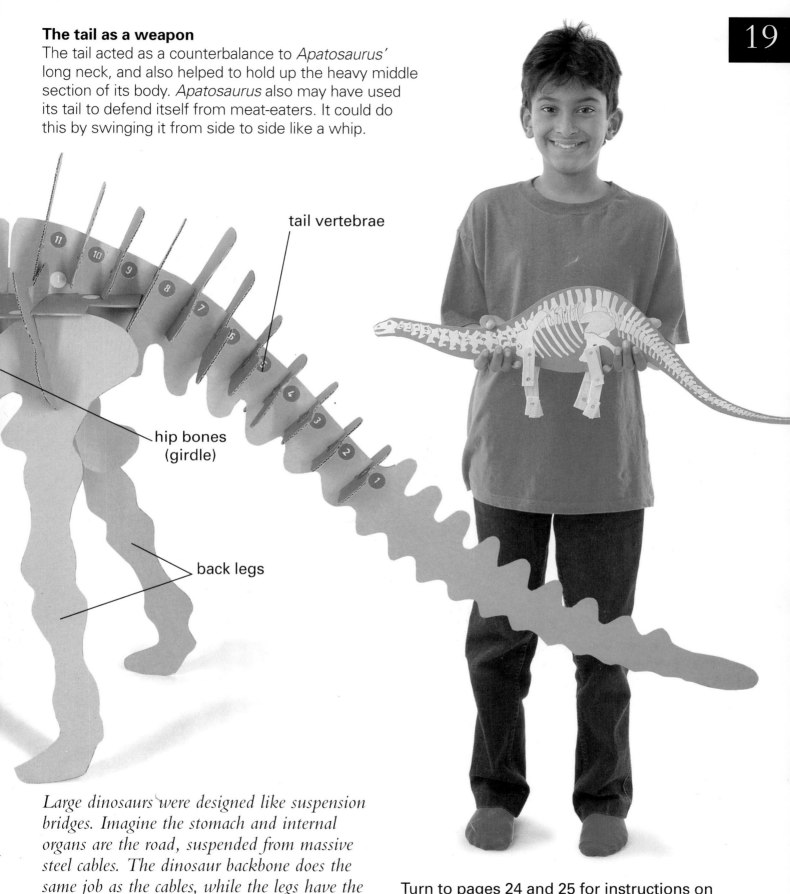

The tail as a weapon
The tail acted as a counterbalance to *Apatosaurus'* long neck, and also helped to hold up the heavy middle section of its body. *Apatosaurus* also may have used its tail to defend itself from meat-eaters. It could do this by swinging it from side to side like a whip.

tail vertebrae

11
10
9
8
7
6
5
4
3
2
1

hip bones (girdle)

back legs

Large dinosaurs were designed like suspension bridges. Imagine the stomach and internal organs are the road, suspended from massive steel cables. The dinosaur backbone does the same job as the cables, while the legs have the same function as bridge supports.

Turn to pages 24 and 25 for instructions on how to make the sauropod model above.

20 Dinosaur Skulls

You can tell a great deal about a dinosaur by looking at its skull. Look at the teeth first: meat-eaters had long, sharp teeth; plant-eaters had shorter, blunt teeth. The jaws are also important: deep jaws mean huge muscles and a powerful bite, typical of the giant meat-eaters.

1 Trace the bone shapes below. Enlarge the lower jaw pieces on a photocopier to around 22 in. long. Enlarge the other pieces by the same percentage. Copy the shapes onto cardboard and cut them out. Take care when cutting out the tabs. Curve the two lower jaw pieces carefully as shown above. Glue the ends together. Slot the lower jaw spacer in the middle and glue in place.

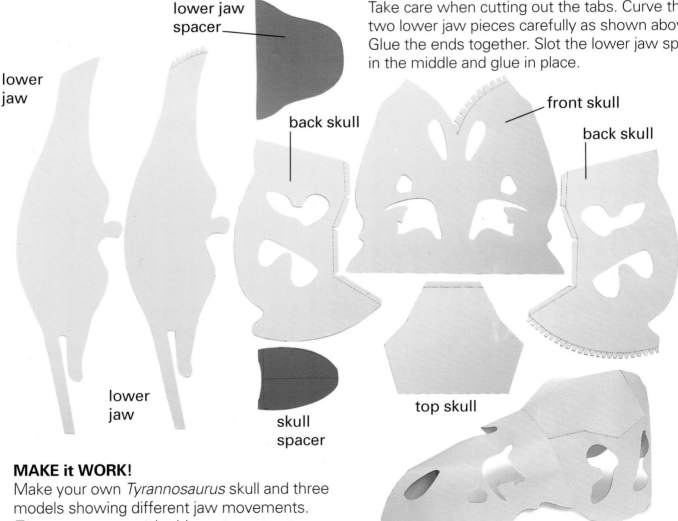

lower jaw spacer

lower jaw

back skull

front skull

back skull

lower jaw

skull spacer

top skull

MAKE it WORK!
Make your own *Tyrannosaurus* skull and three models showing different jaw movements. *Tyrannosaurus* was the biggest meat-eater on land and could have eaten any plant-eater.

You will need
glue

a craft knife

tracing paper

cream, brown and white cardboard

a pencil

scissors

2 Bend the front skull shape in half so that the tabs fit under the opposite side. Glue them in place. Now glue the tab on the top skull to the middle of the front skull. Next, glue the two back skulls to the front and top skull, and to each other. Fit the skull spacer behind nostrils.

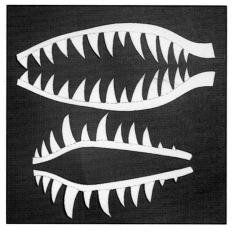

lower

upper

3 Place the skull you have just made on top of the lower jaw. Trace the four rows of teeth above and use a photocopier to enlarge them so that they fit the jaws. Trace them onto white cardboard and cut them out. Glue the longer row of teeth to the upper jaw, and the shorter one to the lower jaw.

Dinosaur jaws
The early reptiles had simple jaws that opened and shut to cut food into pieces. However, both meat-eating and plant-eating dinosaurs had jaws that were shaped and hinged differently from early reptiles. This different design made them much more powerful and efficient.

jaws of a primitive reptile

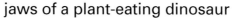

jaws of a plant-eating dinosaur

jaws of a meat-eating dinosaur

You will need
glue	soft wood
a saw	a craft knife
a hand drill	pink and white cardboard

$1/5$ in. dowel rod: 3 dowel rods 1 in. long

To make a primitive reptile's jaws
Cut two pieces of wood $6^1/_2$ in. long. Drill two $1/5$ in. holes in each piece, 2 in. from the ends. Push a piece of dowel rod through the holes to make the hinge as shown. Glue a piece of white cardboard onto the jaws as shown above. This shows where the reptile's bite is strongest.

To make a plant-eater's jaws
Cut wood as above and glue together. Join the jaws with a $1/5$ in. dowel rod. Glue on the pink cardboard as shown. As you can see, these jaws are lower than the hinge point. This gives the plant-eater a more powerful bite along the whole jaw, not just at a single point, as on the primitive reptile's jaw.

To make a meat-eater's jaw
Using wood $12^1/_5$ in. long, make jaws as before. The pink cardboard shows how the jaw is slightly curved. The bite is strongest here, where the largest teeth are. They pierce the flesh of prey.

22 Legs and Posture

Dinosaurs had straight legs that were held underneath the body. This meant they stood fully upright on two or four legs. With straight legs, they could move faster and walk farther than sprawling animals. Also, they were able to grow much larger, because their legs could support a lot of weight.

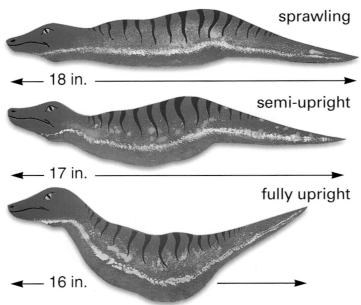

sprawling reptile, such as a modern lizard

MAKE it WORK!

To compare different ways of walking, make models of a **sprawler** (a reptile with arms and legs that stick out sideways), a semi-upright reptile (with legs tucked partly under the body), and an upright dinosaur.

sprawling

← 18 in. →

semi-upright

← 17 in. →

fully upright

← 16 in. →

For the bodies you will need

scissors	pencil
paints and paintbrushes	thick cardboard

1 Draw the three body shapes and cut them out of thick cardboard. Paint the faces and bodies to match the colors shown below.

semi-upright reptile, such as a modern crocodile, or dinosaur **ancestor**

For the sprawling reptile's legs, you will need

a hand drill   glue
$2/3$ in. wide softwood: 12 pieces 2 in. long,
   12 pieces 1 in. long
$1/5$ in. dowel rod: 12 pieces $3/5$ in. long

1 Drill two $1/5$ in. holes in the longer pieces of wood, 0.03 in. from each end. Drill one hole in the shorter pieces, 0.03 in. from one end. Place a 1 in. piece of wood between two 2 in. pieces. Line up the holes and push a dowel rod through. Put one 2 in. piece between the open end of the joined pair and secure with a dowel rod. Sandwich the 2 in. piece between two 1 in. pieces and secure with a dowel rod.

2 Glue the legs to the body. Each leg should sit flat against the body as shown at far left.

For the semi-upright reptile's legs you will need
a hand drill   glue
$2/3$ in. wide softwood: 12 pieces 2 in. long,
  12 pieces 1 in. long
$1/5$ in. dowel rod: 12 pieces $3/5$ in. long

1 Put the legs together as you did for the sprawling reptile. Glue the legs at an angle, so that the body is raised off the ground.

2 For each leg, sandwich one end of a $2^2/3$ in. piece between two $1^1/2$ in. pieces, and the other end between two $3^1/2$ in. pieces. Secure with two $3/5$ in. long pieces of dowel rod.

3 Make two holes in the body for the arms and legs. Push a $1^1/3$ in. length of dowel rod through the open end of the arms, the hole in the body, and the other arm. Repeat this to attach the legs.

Dinosaurs grew very large because of their upright legs. Today's sprawling reptiles cannot hold their bellies off the ground, so they never grow bigger than a lizard.

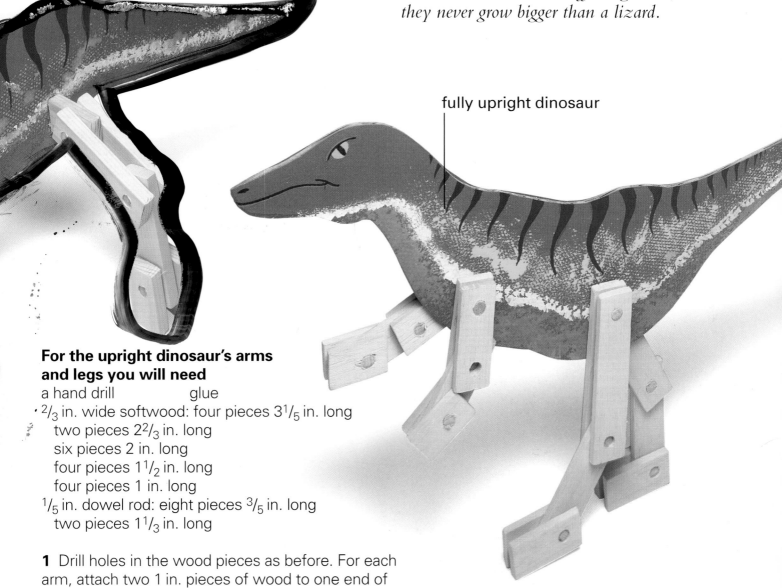

fully upright dinosaur

For the upright dinosaur's arms and legs you will need
a hand drill   glue
$2/3$ in. wide softwood: four pieces $3^1/5$ in. long
  two pieces $2^2/3$ in. long
  six pieces 2 in. long
  four pieces $1^1/2$ in. long
  four pieces 1 in. long
$1/5$ in. dowel rod: eight pieces $3/5$ in. long
  two pieces $1^1/3$ in. long

1 Drill holes in the wood pieces as before. For each arm, attach two 1 in. pieces of wood to one end of a 2 in. piece, and two 2 in. pieces to the other end. Fix with two $3/5$ in. long pieces of dowel rod.

The first dinosaurs stood up on their hind legs. These early dinosaurs were the size of humans and they caught and ate small animals with their hands. Later dinosaurs were much larger and could no longer support all their weight on their hind legs. They had to go down on all fours.

MAKE it WORK!

Make a four-legged (**quadrupedal**) sauropod dinosaur and a two-legged (**bipedal**) ornithopod to see how each dinosaur walked.

You will need

scissors
a hand drill
corrugated cardboard
paints and a paintbrush

For the sauropod you will need

$2/3$ in. wide softwood:
  twelve pieces 2 in. long
  eight pieces 1 in. long
$1/5$ in. dowel rod: eight pieces $3/5$ in. long
  two pieces $1 1/3$ in. long

For the ornithopod you will need

$2/3$ in. wide softwood:
  four pieces 5 in. long
  two pieces $3 1/2$ in. long
  eight pieces 2 in. long
  two pieces $1 2/3$ in. long
  two pieces $1 1/2$ in. long
  four pieces 1 in. long
$1/5$ in. dowel rod:
  two pieces $1 1/3$ in. long
  ten pieces $3/5$ in. long

1 Copying the finished models, draw the ornithopod and sauropod body shapes onto corrugated cardboard. Then cut the shapes out. Trace the skeleton outlines onto the cardboard and paint the bones white or pale yellow.

2 Drill $1/5$ in. holes in all the pieces of wood as shown below at left. To make each sauropod leg, take one 2 in. piece of wood and sandwich it between two 1 in. pieces. Line up the holes and secure with a $3/5$ in. long dowel rod. Now sandwich the free end of the 2 in. piece between two 2 in. pieces. Line up the holes and secure with a $3/5$ in. long dowel rod.

3 Take the open end of each of the sauropod's back legs and secure to the cardboard body with a $1 1/3$ in. long dowel rod. Repeat for the front legs.

4 For each of the ornithopod's arms, take one $1 2/3$ in. piece of wood and sandwich it between two 1 in. pieces. Line up the holes and secure with a $3/5$ in. long dowel rod. Now sandwich the free end of the $1 2/3$ in. piece between two 2 in. pieces. Line up the holes and secure with a $3/5$ in. long dowel rod.

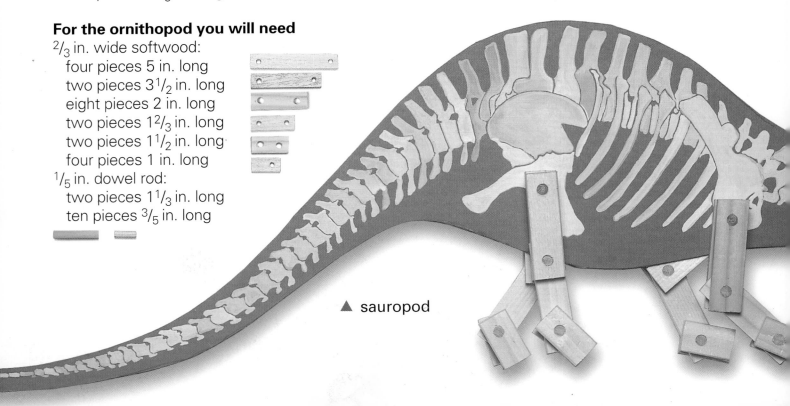

▲ sauropod

5 For each of the ornithopod's legs, take a 1¹/₂ in. piece and sandwich it between two 2 in. pieces. Line up the holes and secure with a ³/₅ in. long dowel rod.

▲ These pictures show the sequence of an ornithopod's stride.

▼ ornithopod

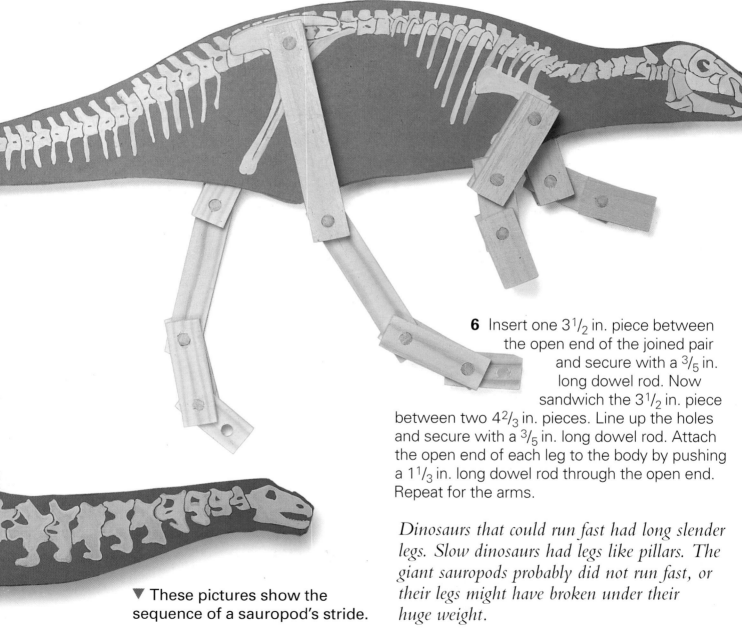

6 Insert one 3¹/₂ in. piece between the open end of the joined pair and secure with a ³/₅ in. long dowel rod. Now sandwich the 3¹/₂ in. piece between two 4²/₃ in. pieces. Line up the holes and secure with a ³/₅ in. long dowel rod. Attach the open end of each leg to the body by pushing a 1¹/₃ in. long dowel rod through the open end. Repeat for the arms.

Dinosaurs that could run fast had long slender legs. Slow dinosaurs had legs like pillars. The giant sauropods probably did not run fast, or their legs might have broken under their huge weight.

▼ These pictures show the sequence of a sauropod's stride.

Some meat-eating dinosaurs used amazing weapons to attack their prey. The **raptors**, a group of human-sized dinosaurs, had a fearsome claw on each back foot. These claws were held up when the animal was attacking, and could be flicked down quickly to tear at flesh.

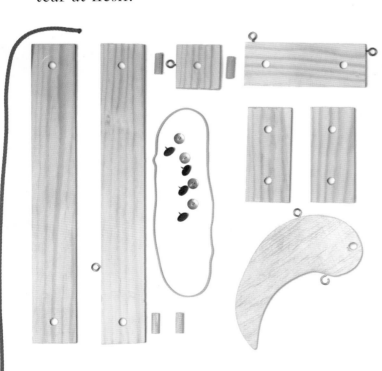

MAKE it WORK!

This flick-claw model is based on *Deinonychus*, a raptor from the early Cretaceous of North America. The model claw is designed to move quickly, just like the real thing.

You will need

a craft knife
$1/5$ in. dowel rod
one brass hook
six brass eyelets
strips of $1/5$ in. softwood:
two long, 10 x $1^1/5$ in.
one medium, 4 x $1^1/5$ in.
two short, 3 x $1^1/5$ in.
one $1^1/5$ in. square balsa-wood claw, $5^1/2$ x $1/5$ in. deep

string
a hand drill
eight pushpins
a long rubber band

1 Ask an adult to help you cut four pieces of dowel rod, $4/5$ in. long. Then drill holes in the pieces of wood, as shown below left. These holes should be $1/5$ in. in diameter, so that the pieces of dowel rod fit into them exactly.

2 Screw the eyelets into the sides of the softwood strips: three on the medium strip, as shown at left, one on a long strip, one on the square piece, and one on the claw's top edge, as shown below. Screw a hook on the underside of the claw, opposite the eyelet.

3 Place a dowel rod into the hole at each end of the long strip with the eyelet. Put a pushpin into each dowel rod on the outside only.

4 Fit the medium strip over the dowel rod at one end of the long strip. Then fit the square at the other end of the long strip, as shown above. Position the short strips at the other end of the medium strip, one on each side. Line up the holes and slot in a piece of dowel rod. Put a pushpin through each end of the dowel rod.

5 Sandwich the claw between the other end of the short strips. Line up the holes and slot in a piece of dowel rod. Secure with a pushpin pushed through both ends.

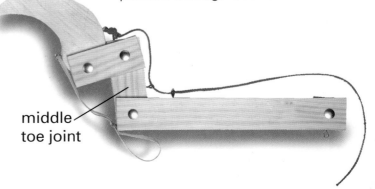

middle toe joint

6 Position the remaining long strip onto the model, as shown below left. Fit onto the dowel rods and secure with pushpins.

7 Thread a long piece of string through the eyelets along the top of the claw, as shown below left. Knot the string at the claw end.

8 Finally, slip the rubber band through the lower eyelet on the middle toe joint. Loop one end onto the hook on the claw and the other end onto the eyelet on the square.

Snapping claws
Now your claw is ready for action! Pull the string until it comes right back, as shown above. Let go of the string and the claw will come down a little. Suddenly, when the rubber band takes over the tension, it will flick down at high speed.

The raptors hunted plant-eating dinosaurs that were often much bigger than themselves. They may have hunted in packs of five or six, chasing a plant-eater until it was exhausted. Then they would leap up at its sides, tearing and slicing at its body with their terrible claws until the beast sank to the ground, finally beaten.

The plant-eating dinosaurs had to find a way of defending themselves from the meat-eating dinosaurs. The large plant-eaters could not escape by running quickly, so many of them developed body armor—bony plates that grew in the skin—to protect themselves.

1 To make the back shield, lie down on a sheet of cardboard and ask a friend to draw around your body. Now copy the shape below left onto the cardboard (use your body outline as a guide to make sure the shield will be large enough to fit on your back). Cut out the shield.

2 Now ask an adult to help you trim the edges with a craft knife. Make sure you cut carefully, so that all the edges are smooth.

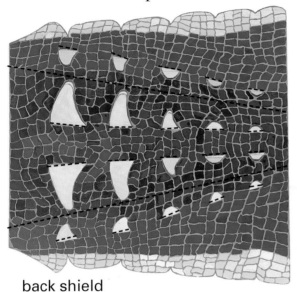

back shield

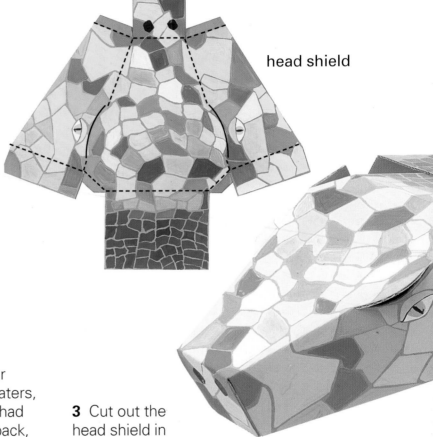

head shield

MAKE it WORK!

Make your own suit of ankylosaur dinosaur armor. The ankylosaurs were large plant-eaters, some of them as big as army tanks. They had bony plates all over their bodies—on the back, around the sides, over the tail, and all over the head. Some ankylosaurs also had a bony club at the end of their tail, which they may have used to fight off meat-eaters.

You will need

string
a pencil
a craft knife
masking tape
paints and paintbrushes
large sheets of cardboard

glue
scissors
paper clips
a long ruler
newspaper

3 Cut out the head shield in proportion to your back shield, as shown above. For the tail, cut a long, thin, triangle shape, as shown above right. Draw some triangular shapes on the body and the tail as shown in the pictures, for the ankylosaur's spines.

4 Draw the bony plate shapes on the back shield and paint them green. Then paint a border of yellow and white scales to show the ankylosaur's underside. Finally, paint the spine shapes pale yellow.

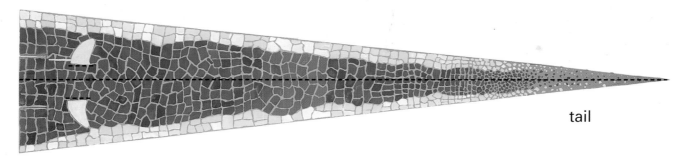

tail

5 Draw bony plate segments on the head shield and paint them in shades of brown. Paint on yellow eyes and black nostrils. Paint the section at the back of the head in green shades. Now paint the tail in shades of green, with the edges (the underside) in yellow. Finally, paint the spine shapes pale yellow.

6 Ask an adult to help you cut around the spine shapes on the back shield and tail. Fold them back along the dotted line, so they stick up.

7 Ask an adult to help you cut a semicircle above the eyes, as marked opposite. Fold the head shield into shape, using a long ruler to help fold along the dotted lines, as shown opposite. Glue the flaps together at the snout. Use paper clips to hold the pieces until the glue is dry. Fold the back shield and tail in the same way.

8 Crumple up some sheets of newspaper into two balls. Wind masking tape around them, then paint them green or blue.

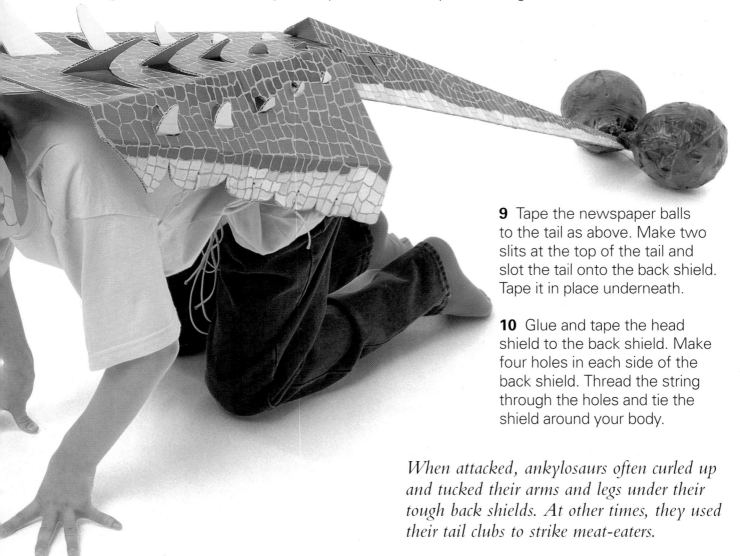

9 Tape the newspaper balls to the tail as above. Make two slits at the top of the tail and slot the tail onto the back shield. Tape it in place underneath.

10 Glue and tape the head shield to the back shield. Make four holes in each side of the back shield. Thread the string through the holes and tie the shield around your body.

When attacked, ankylosaurs often curled up and tucked their arms and legs under their tough back shields. At other times, they used their tail clubs to strike meat-eaters.

30 Dinosaur Speed

The ornithopods, or two-legged plant-eaters, were among the fastest dinosaurs. These long-legged creatures often raced along in herds, reaching speeds of up to 31 miles per hour when they were being chased by meat-eaters. Their long tails helped them keep their balance as they ran.

MAKE it WORK!
Make a model of *Hypsilophodon*—a small ornithopod that lived in the early Cretaceous in southern England. Its relatives lived throughout the world—in Europe, North America, Africa and Australia.

2 Wrap newspaper around the wire body, neck and tail and tape in place. Leave the feet, hands, head, and end of the tail uncovered. At this point, you can keep on bending the wire covered with masking tape until your *Hypsilophodon* looks similar to the one above.

You will need
wire
pliers
plasticine
strips of thin cloth, such as cotton
paints and paintbrushes

scissors
a rolling pin
newspaper
masking tape
plaster of Paris

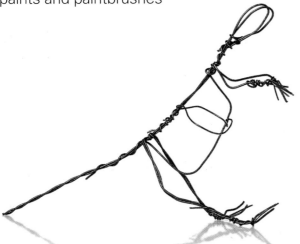

3 Mix some plaster of Paris with water. Make sure the mixture is thick, but not stiff.

1 Using pliers, twist two long lengths of wire together to make the backbone, leaving a loop for the head. Add loops of wire for the ribcage. Twist short lengths of wire onto the backbone for the arms and legs, carefully shaping the ends into five fingers and four toes.

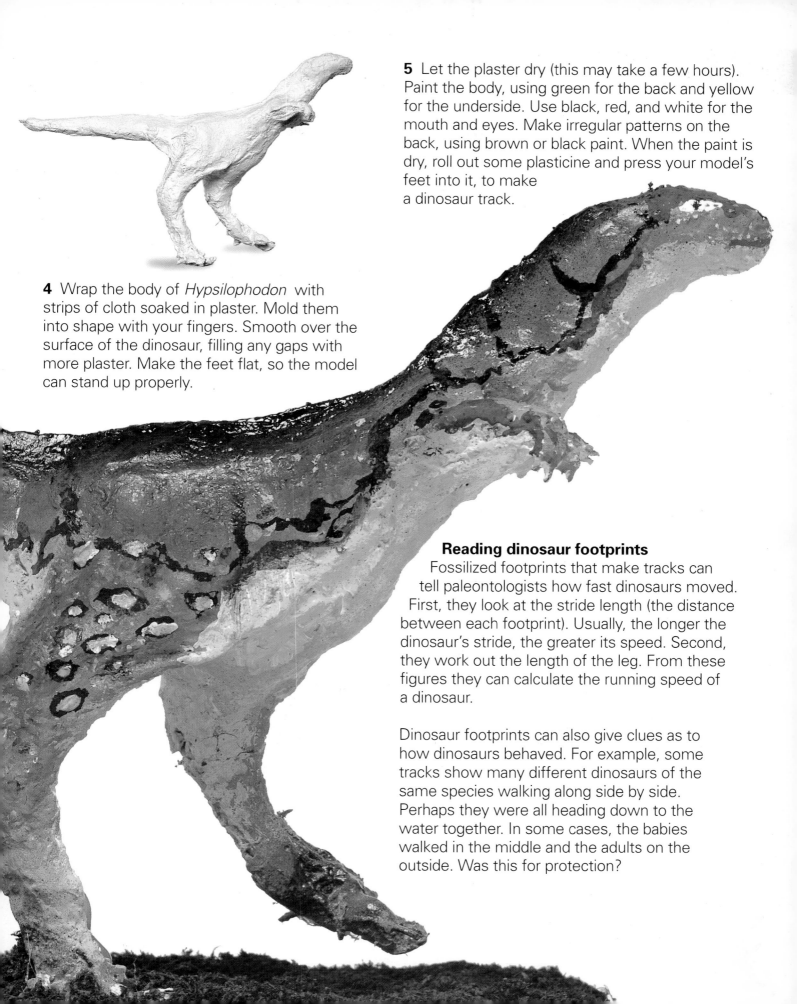

5 Let the plaster dry (this may take a few hours). Paint the body, using green for the back and yellow for the underside. Use black, red, and white for the mouth and eyes. Make irregular patterns on the back, using brown or black paint. When the paint is dry, roll out some plasticine and press your model's feet into it, to make a dinosaur track.

4 Wrap the body of *Hypsilophodon* with strips of cloth soaked in plaster. Mold them into shape with your fingers. Smooth over the surface of the dinosaur, filling any gaps with more plaster. Make the feet flat, so the model can stand up properly.

Reading dinosaur footprints

Fossilized footprints that make tracks can tell paleontologists how fast dinosaurs moved. First, they look at the stride length (the distance between each footprint). Usually, the longer the dinosaur's stride, the greater its speed. Second, they work out the length of the leg. From these figures they can calculate the running speed of a dinosaur.

Dinosaur footprints can also give clues as to how dinosaurs behaved. For example, some tracks show many different dinosaurs of the same species walking along side by side. Perhaps they were all heading down to the water together. In some cases, the babies walked in the middle and the adults on the outside. Was this for protection?

Brachiosaurus was the largest dinosaur. The evidence came from a complete skeleton. It was 82 feet long and probably weighed 55 to 66 short tons. Larger dinosaurs, such as *Supersaurus*, may have weighed twice as much, but no one has found a complete skeleton of this creature.

MAKE it WORK!

Make your own giant sauropod *Brachiosaurus* (in the same way as you made *Hypsilophodon* on pages 30 to 31). Now do an experiment that will tell you the approximate weight of *Brachiosaurus*.

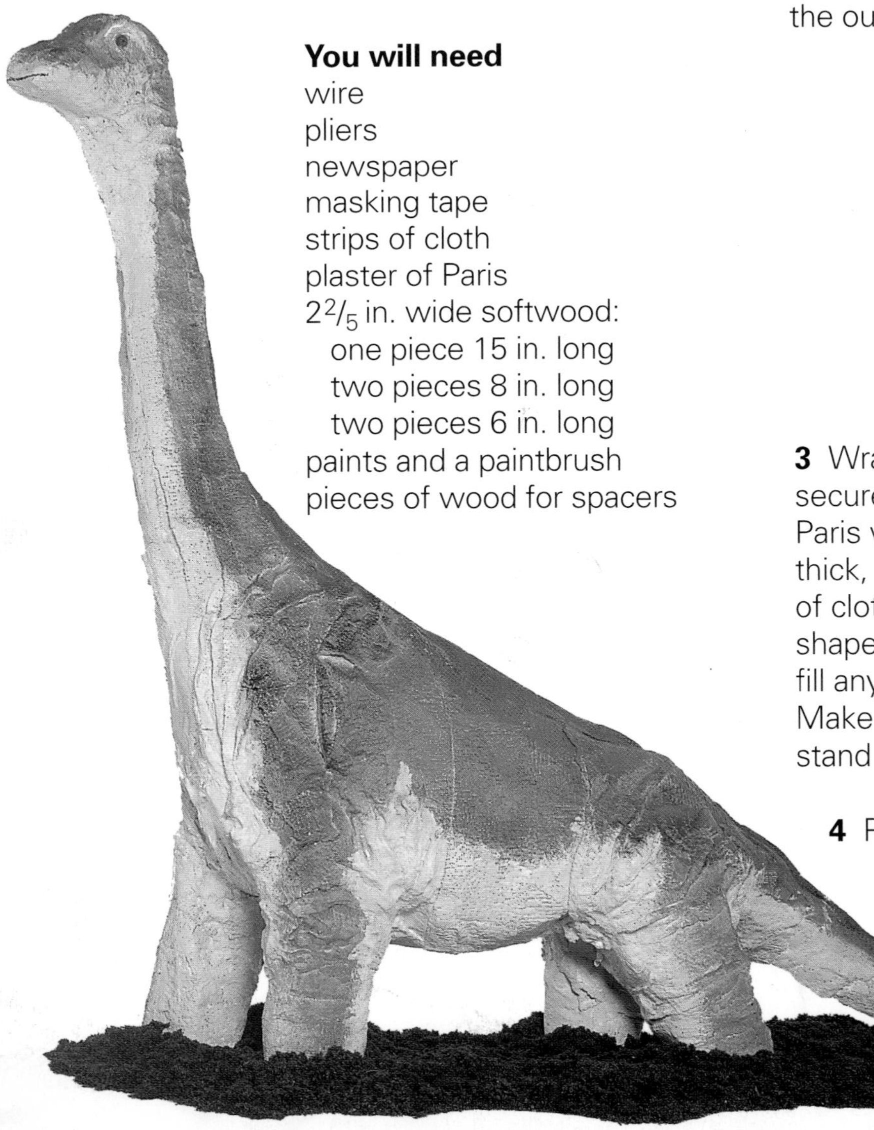

You will need

wire
pliers
newspaper
masking tape
strips of cloth
plaster of Paris
$2\frac{2}{5}$ in. wide softwood:
   one piece 15 in. long
   two pieces 8 in. long
   two pieces 6 in. long
paints and a paintbrush
pieces of wood for spacers

1 For the body, glue two small wood spacers on each side of the 15 in. piece of wood. Add the legs by gluing the four remaining pieces of wood to the spacers, angling one so that it looks like the leg is moving. Make sure the longer legs are at the front.

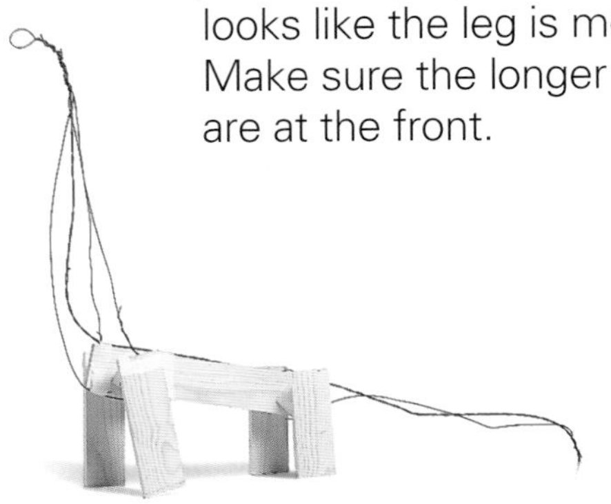

2 Using pliers, twist two lengths of wire together to make the backbone. Tape in place on the wooden body. Make the head by looping a short piece of wire and twisting the ends onto the backbone. Add more pieces of wire to make the outline of the neck and tail. Tape the wire in place as shown above.

3 Wrap newspaper around the frame and secure with tape. Now mix some plaster of Paris with water. Make sure the mixture is thick, but not stiff. Wrap the body with strips of cloth soaked in plaster and mold them into shape with your fingers. Add more plaster to fill any gaps and make a smooth surface. Make the feet flat, so that the dinosaur will stand up. Let it dry.

4 Paint the body of the *Brachiosaurus* gray or dark blue, with a yellow underside. Use black for the mouth and red for the eyes.

Working out the weight

To find out how much *Brachiosaurus* weighed, you will need a plastic model that is accurately modeled on a full-size reconstruction. You also need to know the scale of your plastic model.

1 Put some weighing scales in a large tray. Fill the weighing dish with water right up to the brim. Be careful not to spill any in the tray.

2 Put the dinosaur into the weighing dish and allow the water to flow over the edge into the large tray underneath.

3 Empty the weighing dish. Now pour the the water that spilled into the large tray back into the dish. Write down the weight of this water in ounces. Now multiply the weight of the water by the scaling factor of the dinosaur (x 100, for example), which is usually printed on its stomach. This will give you the approximate weight of the dinosaur in ounces. Now convert this into pounds, or tons.

Sauropods, such as Brachiosaurus, *were ten times bigger than an elephant. Some experts think they were* **cold-blooded**. *Cold-blooded animals need less food and use less energy than* **warm-blooded** *animals do. This is because their body temperature is controlled by how hot or cold it is outside. Warm-blooded animals, such as humans, convert food into energy to heat their bodies from the inside. Some experts say that if* Brachiosaurus *was warm-blooded, it could not have eaten enough to survive.*

Paleontologists have debated whether the dinosaurs were warm-blooded or not. Did dinosaurs have constant body temperatures like birds and **mammals**, or did their body temperatures simply match the air temperature? The bony plates of *Stegosaurus* give us some clues.

MAKE it WORK!

Make a model of the dinosaur *Stegosaurus* and think about how it might have used the bone plates on its back. These plates were set into the skin, rather than into the skeleton.

You will need

wire	plaster of Paris
pliers	cardboard and scissors
newspaper	masking tape and glue
strips of cloth	paints and paintbrushes

1 Twist two pieces of wire together with pliers to make the backbone. For the legs, twist smaller pieces of wire together and attach these to the backbone. Use extra pieces of wire to make the rest of the body shape.

2 Stuff the body and tail with newspaper, then wind masking tape round the body, neck and tail. Fill the shape out to look well rounded.

3 Make up some plaster of Paris, following the instructions on the package. Soak strips of cloth in the mixture. Stretch the cloth strips over the wire frame, building up several layers. Now build up a small head shape with an open mouth, by carefully shaping the damp plaster.

4 Smooth the surface of the model with your fingers to make the correct body shape. Add plaster to fill any gaps, then let it dry.

5 Draw back plates in three different sizes on cardboard and cut them out. Glue the plates along the spine as shown above. Draw four long spikes on cardboard and cut them out. Glue them onto the end of the tail.

6 When your *Stegosaurus* is completely dry, paint it. Use contrasting colors, such as yellow and red, or green and brown. Paint one color all over the body, and let it dry. Then add irregular shapes in another color. You can sprinkle soil or wood shavings around the base of the model if you like.

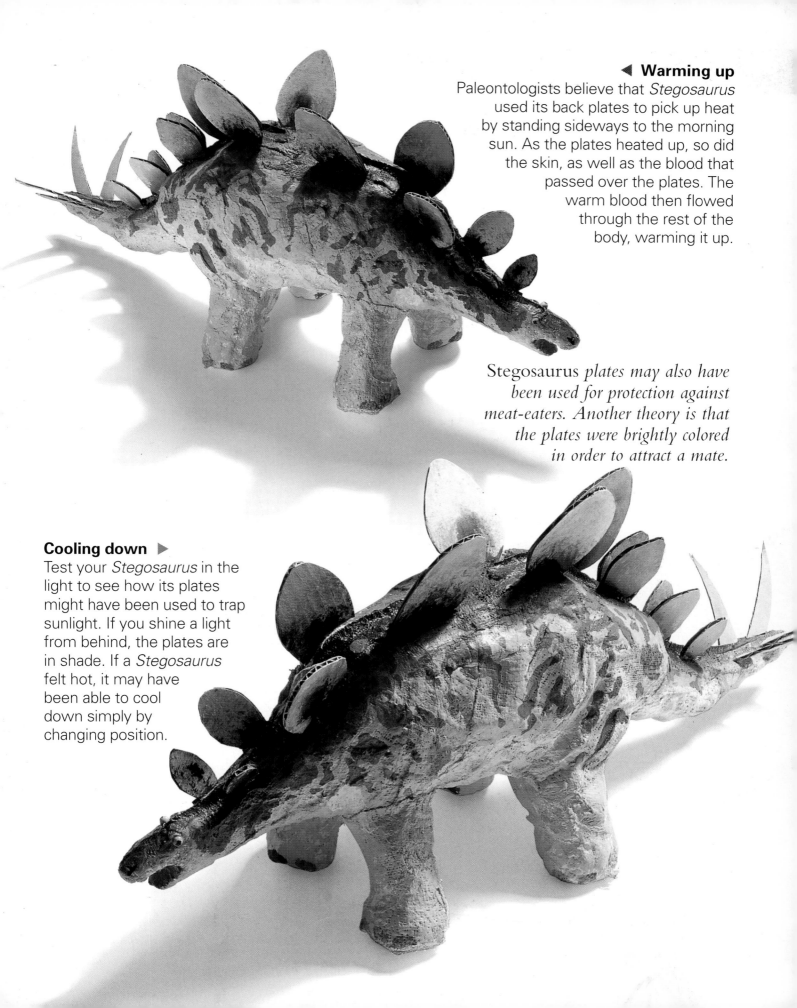

◀ Warming up

Paleontologists believe that *Stegosaurus* used its back plates to pick up heat by standing sideways to the morning sun. As the plates heated up, so did the skin, as well as the blood that passed over the plates. The warm blood then flowed through the rest of the body, warming it up.

Stegosaurus plates may also have been used for protection against meat-eaters. Another theory is that the plates were brightly colored in order to attract a mate.

Cooling down ▶

Test your *Stegosaurus* in the light to see how its plates might have been used to trap sunlight. If you shine a light from behind, the plates are in shade. If a *Stegosaurus* felt hot, it may have been able to cool down simply by changing position.

Like birds and reptiles, dinosaurs laid eggs. They made a nest on the ground and laid 20 or 30 eggs that looked like long, narrow hens' eggs with a hard, chalky shell. Dinosaurs often laid their eggs in mud or sand nests and covered them up to keep them warm and safe from predators.

MAKE it WORK!

Make a model of a *Triceratops* and its nest. *Triceratops* was a ceratopsian or "horned face" dinosaur. Ceratopsians were plant-eaters with horns on their noses and foreheads, which they used to protect themselves from meat-eaters. Their neck frills were thought to act as shields.

You will need

pliers
dried moss
plaster of Paris
scissors and cardboard
paints and paintbrushes

wire
hen's eggs
newspaper
masking tape
strips of cloth

1 Twist two pieces of wire together to make the backbone, the head and the belly, as shown below. Twist two short pieces of wire together for each pair of legs and attach to the body. Now add extra wire to shape the body.

3 Twist two short lengths of wire onto the top of the head to make two long horns. Now add a loop of wire around the back of the head to make the frill. Cover these with pieces of newspaper and masking tape.

2 Stuff the body with crumpled-up newspaper and wind masking tape round the body, neck and tail, as shown above right. Make the body round, and make the head with an open mouth.

4 Make up some plaster of Paris and soak strips of cloth in the mixture. Make sure the plaster is runny, but not stiff. Stretch the cloth over the wire frame and build up several layers. Add more plaster to fill in any gaps.

5 Continue adding plaster around the horns, so that they are rounded. Smooth the surface of the model with your fingers to make the correct body shape, as shown below left. Using stiff plaster, add a short horn to the nose and a hooked beak to the mouth.

8 Use green and yellow paint to give your *Triceratops* model a thick, scaly skin. Paint the horns, edges of the frill, toes and underside in yellow and white. Use brown and black for the eyes, and red and white for the tongue and teeth.

9 Make a *Triceratops'* nest from dried moss. Put several hens' eggs in the nest and place the nest next to your finished model.

In life, *Triceratops* measured up to $29\frac{1}{2}$ ft. long. Their eggs were a maximum 12 in. long, a little larger than an ostrich egg. In our model below, the eggs are much larger than they should be in proportion to the model.

6 Using stiff plaster that has nearly dried out, shape five toes on each foot. Do this carefully, so that the *Triceratops* will stand properly. Roll up two tiny balls of newspaper for the eyes and press into the plaster. Let the plaster dry.

7 To finish the frill, cut out several triangle shapes from cardboard. Glue these around the neck shield as shown above. Let the glue dry.

Some dinosaur babies could run about and find food almost as soon as they hatched. Others had to wait in the nest for their parents to feed them. Paleontologists discovered this when they studied nesting sites in the state of Montana and in Mongolia. They found bones of parents and one-year-olds near the nests, along with the remains of leaves and berries.

Dinosaurs had small, reptile-sized brains (a bird or a mammal the size of a dinosaur would have a brain 10 times as big). The dinosaur brain was good enough to tell them where to find food and how to escape danger, but they were unable to learn as well as birds and mammals. Only the small meat–eaters, such as the raptors (see pages 26 to 27) had as much brain power as birds.

1 Twist two long pieces of wire together to make the backbone, tail and a head with an open mouth. Then twist two smaller pieces of wire together for the arms and legs. Attach these by twisting them around the backbone. Now add more pieces of wire to fill in the body, as shown below left.

2 Stuff the body, neck and head with crumpled-up newspaper. Wind masking tape around the body, head, and neck, as well as the upper part of the legs and the tail.

MAKE it WORK!
Make a model of *Tyrannosaurus*, the biggest meat-eating dinosaur. Although *Tyrannosaurus* had a huge body, its brain was much smaller than yours. Like all dinosaurs, its brain was protected by a tough, bony case.

3 Make up some plaster of Paris and soak strips of cloth in the mixture. Stretch these over the wire frame and build up several layers of strips over the whole body as shown below. Make sure the model can stand upright.

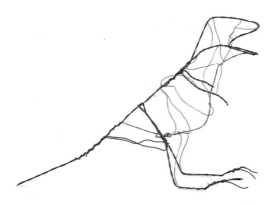

You will need
wire
scissors
craft knife
masking tape
strips of cloth
plaster of Paris

pliers
newspaper
toothpicks
two large plastic beads
paints and paintbrushes

4 To make the teeth, cut several toothpicks, into short points. Push these firmly into the damp plaster around the edges of the mouth. Let the plaster dry.

5 Paint the *Tyrannosaurus* in shades of orange, red, brown, and black, or colors of your choice. Use bright red for the mouth. You can paint on the eyes, or glue on two large plastic beads. Sprinkle soil or wood shavings around the base.

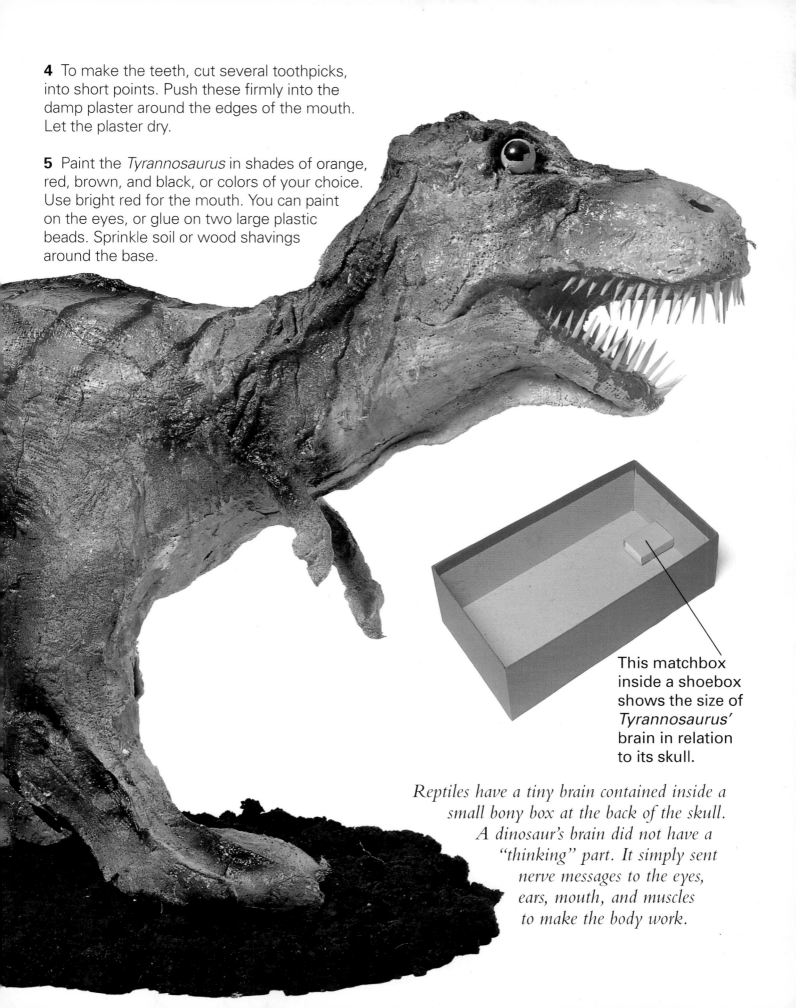

This matchbox inside a shoebox shows the size of *Tyrannosaurus'* brain in relation to its skull.

Reptiles have a tiny brain contained inside a small bony box at the back of the skull. A dinosaur's brain did not have a "thinking" part. It simply sent nerve messages to the eyes, ears, mouth, and muscles to make the body work.

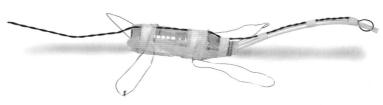

Dinosaurs lived only on land. However, there were giant reptiles in the seas during the time of the dinosaurs. The most unusual were the **plesiosaurs**, which had broad bodies, and long necks and tails. The plesiosaurs swam by using their broad limbs as huge paddles.

MAKE it WORK!

Plesiosaurs were reptiles, which means that they had to breathe air. They could probably have remained underwater for up to 10 minutes in search of fish to eat, but then they had to surface for air. We show you how to make your own plesiosaur—this one sinks and swims!

2 Pierce a hole in the lid of the bottle, thread in the plastic tube, and fix the tube to the neck with tape. The other end of the tube should reach right to the head, as shown above.

3 Bend some wire into paddle shapes for the plesiosaur's limbs, as above. Tape them in place under the bottle. Wrap newspaper around the neck, body, and tail, twisting it tightly to get a neat shape. Tape the newspaper firmly in place.

You will need
wire
pliers
a plastic tube
masking tape
strips of cloth
a plastic bottle with lid

paints
varnish
scissors
newspaper
plaster of Paris

1 Fold a long piece of wire in half, and twist it together with pliers, leaving a loop for the head. The twisted wire will be the backbone. Now fix the plastic bottle below the backbone, about halfway along with masking tape. Make sure the bottle top points to the mouth.

4 Cover the whole body with cloth strips soaked in plaster of Paris. Mold carefully around the head, body and tail, so that your model looks like the one above. Leave an opening in the mouth for the end of the tube and take care not to let any plaster block it up.

5 Let the plaster dry. Paint the plesiosaur, using green or blue for the back, and yellow for the belly. You can add rough stripes or spots to the back. This color pattern acts as camouflage in the water. Once the paint is dry, apply four coats of varnish. Allow plenty of drying time between each coat.

Plesiosaurs moved their paddles down and backward to push themselves forward in the water. Then they turned the paddle so that the narrow side faced forward, and brought it up to the front again. The tip of the paddle followed a figure-of-eight pattern, like the wing of a bird in flight. Penguins use a similar paddle action when they swim.

Taking a dive

Make your plesiosaur sink by filling it with water. Simply place it underwater or carefully pour water into a funnel fitted into the plastic tube. Your model will float when there is no water in the bottle—use the plastic tube for pouring water out. When real plesiosaurs wanted to dive, they probably blew all the air out of their lungs to make themselves heavier. When they were breathing normally at the surface, they floated.

Pterosaurs were neither dinosaurs nor birds. They belonged to the archosaur group and were perhaps related to the dinosaurs. They ruled the skies when the dinosaurs ruled the Earth—from the late Triassic to the end of the Cretaceous, the time of the great **extinction** (see pages 44 to 45). Some, such as *Pteranodon*, were huge, with a wingspan of 26 feet.

1 Trace all the body and wing parts below. Ask an adult to enlarge the wings on a photocopier, until they measure around 20 in. long. Enlarge the other pieces by the same percentage.

2 Tape the photocopy onto the cardboard. Ask an adult to help you cut out the shapes with a craft knife. Make sure the grooves in the cardboard run along the length of the wings.

3 Cut slits into the cardboard shapes, as shown below. They must be wide enough for the shapes to fit together firmly.

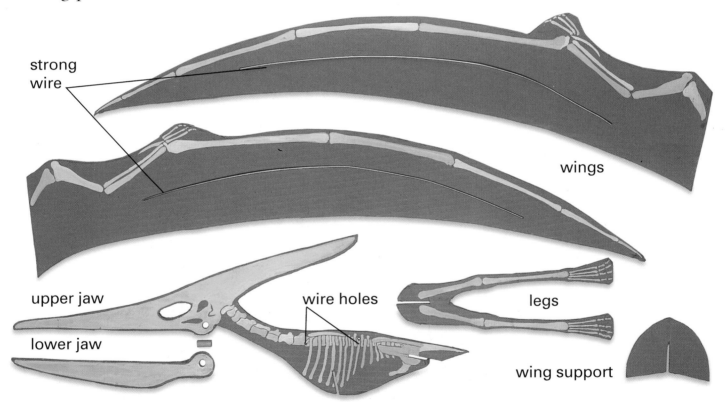

strong wire

wings

upper jaw

lower jaw

wire holes

legs

wing support

MAKE it WORK!
You can make a gliding model of *Pteranodon* (in life, it flapped its wings, like a giant bird).

You will need
plasticine
two strong wires
a 1/5 in. dowel rod
corrugated cardboard
paints and a paintbrush

a pencil
a craft knife
glue and tape
tracing paper
a bradawl

4 Paint the *Pteranodon* skeleton onto the cardboard, using the picture above as a guide. Trace the shapes in pencil first and then paint bone shapes either cream or yellow. Ask an adult to help you cut out an eye socket and a 1/5 in. hole in the upper and lower jaws. Use the bradawl to make two small wire holes in the backbone, as shown.

5 Fit the *Pteranodon* jaws together by lining up the holes and pushing the dowel rod through. Make sure the jaw can open and shut (it must stay shut when the animal flies). Slot the legs into place.

6 Push the supporting wires into the cardboard grooves inside one wing, from the straight edge (see the arrows on the picture at left for the correct position). To attach the wing to the body, thread the wires through the holes in the backbone. Now push the wires into the remaining wing, as before. Finally, fix the wing support into the slot below the ribs.

7 Now you are ready to launch your *Pteranodon*. Keep the jaws closed and hold it underneath the wings. If the head dips, add a piece of plasticine to the tail. If the tail dips, add a piece of plasticine to the head.

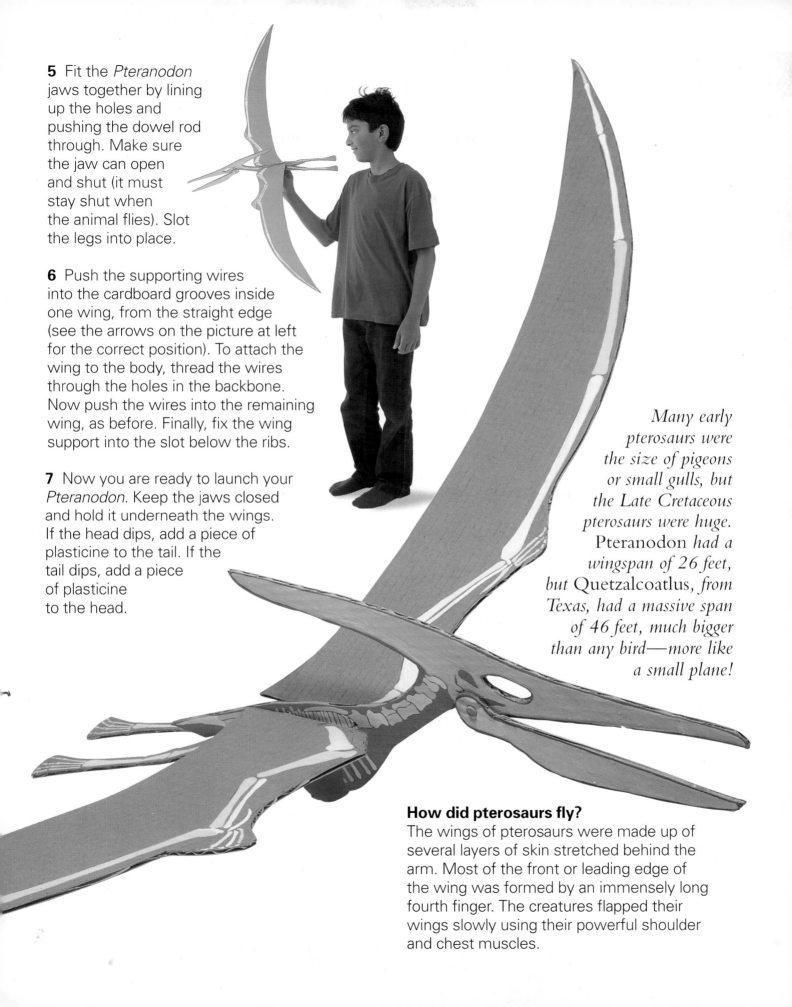

Many early pterosaurs were the size of pigeons or small gulls, but the Late Cretaceous pterosaurs were huge. Pteranodon had a wingspan of 26 feet, but Quetzalcoatlus, from Texas, had a massive span of 46 feet, much bigger than any bird—more like a small plane!

How did pterosaurs fly?
The wings of pterosaurs were made up of several layers of skin stretched behind the arm. Most of the front or leading edge of the wing was formed by an immensely long fourth finger. The creatures flapped their wings slowly using their powerful shoulder and chest muscles.

Sixty-five million years ago, the dinosaurs died out. There have been many theories about this great extinction. Some scientists believe the climate changed from warm to cold. Others think the Earth was hit by a giant **meteorite** that sent up clouds of dust and blacked out the sun.

MAKE it WORK!

You can make a game to re-create the extinction of the dinosaurs. Throughout the game, players lose dinosaurs, trees and bushes until all that's left is a barren, volcanic landscape.

You will need

glue	thin tape
a pencil	scissors
colored cardboard	plasticine
a pencil sharpener	paper clips
baseboard 19 x 19 in.	a long ruler
paints and a paintbrush	tracing paper
thick and thin dowel rods	white stickers

1 Cut out $4/5$ in. strips of thin red, white, blue and green cardboard. Glue these to the borders of the baseboard. Now make a grid of $1\frac{1}{2}$ in. squares. This will make 11 squares along each side. Using a ruler and a pencil, join up the marks so that you end up with 121 squares, each measuring $1\frac{1}{2}$ x $1\frac{1}{2}$ in.

2 Copy the volcano shape shown above. Cut out the shape from cardboard and bend the edges along the fold lines as above. Make one large volcano (to occupy nine squares), two medium (four squares), and three small (one square).

3 Glue the volcano shapes together (secure with paper clips until the glue dries). Paint the volcanoes white with red and orange lava.

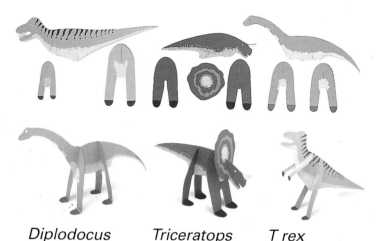

Diplodocus   Triceratops   T rex

4 To make the dinosaurs, trace the shapes as above. Enlarge the tracings about 300 per cent, so that each dinosaur fits inside one square. Copy the shapes onto cardboard and cut them out. Make slits in the legs and bodies, then slot them together. Paint the models and bend their feet so that they can stand. Each player should have three plant-eaters (one *Triceratops* and two *Diplodocus*) and one meat-eater, *Tyrannosaurus rex*.

5 Make five palm trees and six bushes. Cut palm fronds from cardboard and glue to lengths of thin dowel rod. Fix the palms to the baseboard with plasticine. Make bushes by sticking leaf shapes to pieces of thick dowel rod as shown above. Cut a pond shape out of blue cardboard.

6 Make the spinner as shown above. Sharpen one end of a thin dowel rod with a pencil sharpener and push it through the middle of the spinner. The spinner will spin on the sharp end.

Playing the game:

1 Up to four people can play the game. Each player takes one side of the board. Place the pond in position on the board, then make a pile of bushes, palms and volcanoes. Players take turns removing one of these from the pile and placing them on the board.

3 The player spins the spinner and moves a dinosaur along that number of squares, in any direction. If the dinosaur lands on a square with a tree or bush, it can remove it. A meat-eater can remove a plant-eater or another meat-eater by landing on its square. If a plant-eater lands on a meat-eater's square, it will be eaten.

2 When the landscape is complete, players take turns placing their dinosaurs on the board. Place your meat-eater last and try to put it next to a plant-eater, so it can eat it! The last person to place a dinosaur on the board starts.

4 The game ends when there are no dinosaurs or plants left on the board. The volcanoes stay on the board all the time (a dinosaur must move around the volcanoes and the pond). The player who ends up with the greatest number of plants and dinosaurs is the winner.

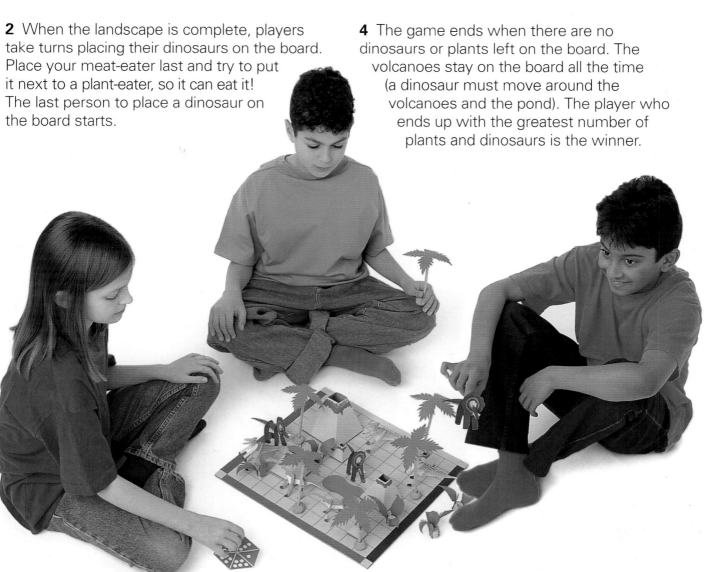

Ammonite A swimming shellfish with a curved shell. It was common in the Jurassic.

Ancestor An early type of animal from which another, later type of animal is descended.

Ankylosauria A dinosaur subgroup containing armored plant-eating dinosaurs, such as *Euoplocephalus*.

Archosauria A group of animals containing archosaurs, the "ruling reptiles." The archosaur group includes dinosaurs, crocodiles, pterosaurs and birds.

Bipedal Walking on two legs, like humans and many dinosaurs.

Cell A unit of living matter so small that it can be seen only under a microscope.

Ceratopsia A dinosaur subgroup containing ceratopsians, or "horn-faced" creatures, such as *Triceratops*.

Cold-blooded An animal, such as a reptile, that has no internal way to control its body temperature. Instead, it heats itself by basking in the sun.

Cretaceous
The period from 145 million to 65 million years ago. The last dinosaurs lived during this time.

Dinosaur An extinct reptile and member of the Dinosauria, a group of generally large, land-living reptiles that had straight limbs.

Excavate To dig up the soil carefully in order to find buried objects, such as skeletons. It may take paleontologists several months to excavate a complete dinosaur skeleton.

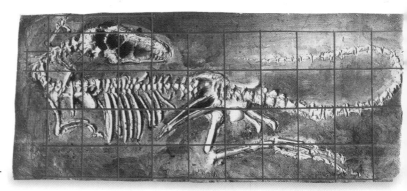

Extinction The death of a species. A mass extinction takes place when many species, like the dinosaurs, die off at the same time.

Fossil The remains of a once living thing, usually preserved in rock.

Genus A group of closely related species.

Geological Relating to the study of rocks and other substances that make up the Earth's crust. Dinosaur fossils preserved in rock can be dated by finding out the age of the rock.

Jurassic The second period in the age of the dinosaurs, from 205 million to 145 million years ago. Ammonites and plesiosaurs were common in seas during this time. It was also the time when dinosaurs reached their largest sizes.

Ligament A tough tissue that connects bones and muscles in the body.

Mammal An animal that has hair and is warm-blooded. Mammals feed their young on milk. Humans, dogs, cats, horses, bats and whales are all mammals.

Mesozoic The era of geological time, from 250 million to 65 million years ago, which includes the Triassic, Jurassic and Cretaceous periods. It is also known as the Age of the Dinosaurs.

Meteorite The remains of a rock from space that has burned up on entering the Earth's atmosphere.

Mineral Any substance found in the earth that is not a vegetable substance. Common minerals are calcite and quartz.

Ornithischian A "bird-hipped" dinosaur that is a member of the suborder Ornithischia. Ornithischians include the plant-eating ornithopods, ceratopsians, stegosaurs and ankylosaurs.

Ornithopoda A group of two-legged, plant-eating dinosaurs with many rows of grinding teeth, such as *Hypsilophodon*.

Paleontologist A person who studies fossils.

Plesiosaur A sea reptile of Jurassic and Cretaceous times. It was an air-breathing animal that ate fish and laid its eggs on land.

Prosauropoda A group of medium-sized, plant-eating dinosaurs with long necks, such as *Plateosaurus*.

Pterosaur A flying reptile with leathery wings stretched along elongated fingers. Pterosaurs lived during the Triassic, Jurassic and Cretaceous periods.

Quadrupedal Walking on all fours.

Raptor A small hunting dinosaur with a curved claw, such as *Deinonychus*.

Reptile An animal with scaly skin and four legs that usually lives on land. Turtles, lizards, crocodiles and snakes are all modern reptiles.

Saurischian A "lizard-hipped" dinosaur that belongs to the suborder Saurischia.

Sauropod A giant, long-necked, plant-eating dinosaur, such as *Brachiosaurus*.

Sauropodomorpha A group of long-necked, plant-eating dinosaurs, most of which walked on all fours.

Skeleton The bony framework that supports animals' bodies and protects delicate organs, such as the heart.

Species A group of plants or animals whose members share the same characteristics and can breed together successfully.

Sprawler An animal that walks with its limbs stuck out to the side, such as a lizard.

Stegosauria A group of "plated", plant-eating dinosaurs, such as *Stegosaurus*.

Theropod A dinosaur that belonged to the Saurischia group. They were all bipedal meat-eaters.

Triassic The period from 250 million to 205 million years ago. Evidence of the first dinosaurs dates from this period.

Warm-blooded A type of animal that can keep its body temperature constant by using heat generated inside itself.

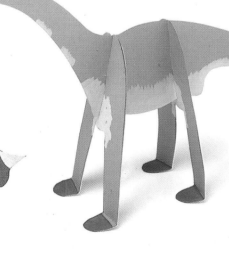

Nicole